Lessons in Losing

Lessons in Losing

RAY MILLER

RESOURCE *Publications* • Eugene, Oregon

LESSONS IN LOSING

Copyright © 2022 Ray Miller. All rights reserved. Except for brief quotations in critical publications or reviews, no part of this book may be reproduced in any manner without prior written permission from the publisher. Write: Permissions, Wipf and Stock Publishers, 199 W. 8th Ave., Suite 3, Eugene, OR 97401.

Resource Publications
An Imprint of Wipf and Stock Publishers
199 W. 8th Ave., Suite 3
Eugene, OR 97401

www.wipfandstock.com

PAPERBACK ISBN: 978-1-6667-4123-0
HARDCOVER ISBN: 978-1-6667-4124-7
EBOOK ISBN: 978-1-6667-4125-4

05/10/22

This book is dedicated to everyone who has felt that their heart has been ripped out through the loss of a loved one and who has said, "Why, God?"

May the Lord bring healing, a new heart, and a new season of hope to you.

Contents

List of Illustrations | ix

Introduction | xi

Prologue: A New Season | 1

    1   What it's All About | 5
    2   Why, God? | 10
    3   Do Not Forsake Me When I Am Old | 14
    4   What Is Ministry? | 18
    5   God's Grace to Us | 22
    6   God's Support Group | 27
    7   Lord, Teach Me to Pray | 31
    8   Getting Rid of Stuff | 36
    9   I'm Not Sure If God Can Use You | 40
    10   What Does it Mean to Be Human? | 45
    11   Jesus Wept | 50
    12   Thank You That She Is with You | 54

Epilogue: The Injustice of a Painless Life | 59

After a Year Has Passed

Introduction | 65

    13   Reflections on a Year of Grieving | 66
    14   To Re- or Not to Re-: That is the Question | 71
    15   It's Still Pretty Much the Same | 76
    16   Deciding to Go Forward | 80

17 Going Political—Kind Of | 85
18 From Real to More Real | 90

Epilogue: Jesus Never Changes | 95

List of Illustrations

Wife of the Year Award, 1979 | 2
Working in church office, early 1980s | 3
Ray, BC | 6
Ray, AD | 6
Deborah and my friend Mike, who both prayed for me to know Jesus | 8
Birthday card from Filipino friend | 11
Our wedding, 1975 | 12
Sparta, Michigan early 1980s | 15
During forty-second anniversary outing | 16
Little Debbie | 19
Spending time with one of her favorite people | 21
Member of high school marching band | 23
With children of Filipino friends | 25
College graduation, 1980 | 28
Medical outreach in the Philippines | 29
Mio, Michigan early 1980s | 32
With members of her children's ministry team in the Philippines | 34
Sophomore high school picture | 37
Business card as interim director of children's home in Philippines | 38
With one of the faithful farm dogs | 41
With her Dad and our kids | 43
At her parents' house in Lansing, Michigan 1980s | 46
With Allen in Pennsylvania late 1970s | 48
With Allen in the Texas bluebonnets, late 1970s | 51

Children's ministry seminar in the Philippines | 52
My "praying Grandma" as a child | 56
With her Dad and Ginger | 57
Enjoying time with a Filipino baby | 60
Our nursery in Mio, Michigan early 1980s | 61
Sitting on a trestle bridge in Eaton Rapids, Michigan 1975 | 67
In Michigan's Upper Peninsula 2017 | 68
Holding one of our kitties in the Philippines | 72
Foster care office that provided housing for her as a child | 74
Fifth grade school picture | 77
Fixing dinner in Mio, Michigan early 1980s | 79
Picnic in Grand Rapids, Michigan mid-1980s | 81
With friends in the Philippines | 83
In the little red wagon on the farm | 86
At the wedding of Filipino friends | 88
With Allen in Texas late 1970s | 91
With Jen in Sparta, Michigan mid-1980s | 93

Introduction

I DIDN'T WRITE THIS book as some kind of professional. There are plenty of resources out there that are written from clinical, pastoral, theological, and other perspectives. Although I am a minister and have served as a pastor and missionary since 1980, my intention was not to write exclusively from that background.

My hope is that you will hear the heart of someone who has gone through the process of caring for and losing a loved one, the process that I'm discussing in the book. If the Holy Spirit can use any of these thoughts to bring comfort, insight, strength, practical wisdom, and so on to you, then I will consider that to be His stamp of approval on this labor of love.

Please be aware that at the same time I have written from an unapologetic Christian and biblical perspective. That is the only lens through which I know or desire to live and to understand the world and my experiences in it.

Although I have experienced some healing and therapeutic benefits from writing this, such was not really my aim in doing so. First, I clearly sensed that God was directing me to do it. Second, it was to provide encouragement to others who are or will be affected by the loss of a loved one.

At the beginning of my writing, I was not sure whether or not to include pictures. They are personal, and in many ways are how I want to remember Deborah until I see her again in heaven. But I have decided that since pictures of loved ones are such a valuable possession to those left behind, I should include a couple of pictures in each Chapter. I also felt it would be beneficial to include study/ reflection questions at the end of each Chapter.

Prologue

A New Season

You husbands in the same way, live with *your wives* in an understanding way, as with someone weaker, *since she is* a woman; and show her honor as a fellow heir of the grace of life, so that your prayers will not be hindered (1 Pet 3:7).[1]

I REMEMBER IT WELL. November 19, 2015. It was my prayer retreat.

During Deborah's and my years of ministry together I tried to regularly set aside times to have a personal prayer retreat. An important part of doing a prayer retreat was to listen to what God was saying to me and to record it in a journal. Prayer retreats were times when God would speak to me about immediate situations and needs and give me wisdom about how to work through them. But they were also times when He would speak to me about larger and longer-term issues.

Deborah and I were in the midst of an intense and challenging time of ministry in the fall of 2015. It was a season filled with questions about the direction God had for us as a couple. Some of the questions were brought to the forefront through rocky ministry relationships and hard-to-navigate situations. Some were also because in retrospect I know now that I had begun to see changes in the woman I had loved and shared life with for four decades.

As I sat, knelt, walked, sang, read Scripture, prayed, and waited quietly throughout the first part of this particular prayer retreat, it seemed that

---

1. All biblical citations are from the *New American Standard Bible* (NASB).

Lessons in Losing

God wasn't saying anything to me. Or at least anything that I could understand. In such times I need a while to tune in my heart, mind, and emotions to what the Lord is trying to say to me. Sometimes I seem to be able to almost immediately sense His direction for the prayer time or retreat. On November 19, I realized that it might take a little while.

After I had prayed and worshiped for an hour or two, I felt the need to just be quiet. My heart finally seemed ready to hear what the Holy Spirit wanted to communicate to me. It was a very simple message: "I am bringing you into a new season. I am going to give you the privilege of serving and loving your wife in a way that you have never had the opportunity to do before." It was just that simple.

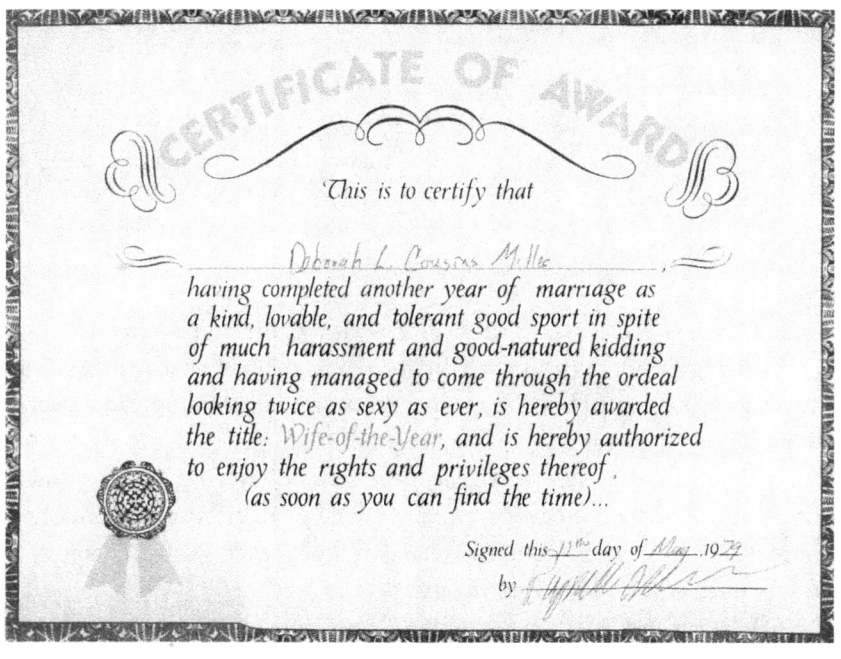

Wife of the Year Award, 1979

Deborah had always been an independent kind of person. Throughout our life together she had worked at many kinds of jobs that demanded resilience, a quick mind, and creativity. In the 1970s and 1980s she worked as a nurse aide, as a computerized embroidery machine operator, and as a long-distance telephone operator in the midst of the massive technological shifts in communications in the 1980s. In the 1990s and until we moved overseas in 2002, she worked as a church office manager, adult foster care home manager, and telephone service representative for a large financial institution.

Deborah also loved hobbies that required discipline, focus, and dedication—sewing and quilting, along with scrap booking and photography. Several times over the years she had also solo driven long road trips with our kids and other relatives.

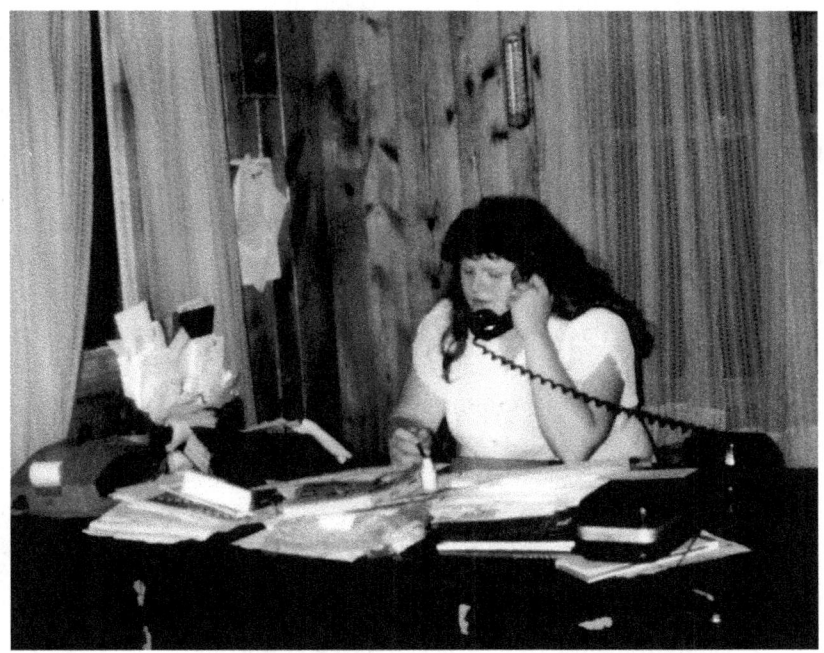

Working in church office, early 1980s

Now, in late 2015, she was starting to struggle with tasks and responsibilities that I had seen her routinely and easily accomplish. In the past she had done many of them much better than I ever could. Now she was beginning to change from that creative, skilled, resilient person to someone for whom everyday tasks were becoming more and more challenging.

Two specific moments earlier in life had always stuck with me. For the longest time I could not understand these moments and why I never seemed to be able to forget them.

In the first one, God seemed to speak very clearly to me as a young believer (maybe eighteen or nineteen years old) that someday I would minister to the elderly. You can imagine that as a youthful believer with a fresh, transforming, and exciting experience with God, such a promise wasn't a source of great excitement to me. But as the years passed, I never seemed to be able to forget that strong impression.

The second moment occurred in late 2002 or early 2003. It involved watching a video entitled *A Vow to Cherish*,[2] made by the Billy Graham organization. It was about a Christian couple, and the wife was diagnosed with Alzheimer's. I remember thinking and praying in my heart, "Lord, please don't ever let that happen to us! I could never handle it."

Everything began to make sense on November 19, 2015. Everything also began to not make sense on that day.

What made sense? The truth that God sees the beginning and end of our lives, and everything in between. That He is faithfully at work in the moments and processes of our lives to bring about the fulfillment of His will. That nothing in all the unpredictability and uncertainty of our lives ever takes Him by surprise. That He is somehow in it all and overseeing it all.

What didn't make sense? I had a lot of questions. They could all pretty much be summarized in one short, anguished phrase: "Lord, why?"

God is under no obligation to justify His ways to us. But He does often answer our "Lord, why?" questions in His own way and time . . .

FOR STUDY AND REFLECTION

1. Why is it important to believe that God knows the whole stream of a person's life?

2. What are some ways that you can deal emotionally with the changes that you see in a loved one who is experiencing a degenerative disease or condition?

3. As you look back at your life, what moments or times can you recognize when God was preparing you for a season of caring for a loved one and/or grieving their loss?

4. How do you find yourself responding spiritually, emotionally, and intellectually to the idea that God is not under obligation to explain or justify to us the things that He does or allows to happen?

---

2. *A Vow to Cherish* (billygraham.org)

Chapter 1

What it's All About

Therefore if anyone is in Christ, *this person is* a new creation; the old things passed away; behold, new things have come. Now all *these* things are from God, who reconciled us to Himself through Christ and gave us the ministry of reconciliation, namely, that God was in Christ reconciling the world to Himself, not counting their wrongdoings against them, and He has committed to us the word of reconciliation. Therefore, we are ambassadors for Christ, as though God were making an appeal through us; we beg you on behalf of Christ, be reconciled to God. He made Him who knew no sin *to be* sin in our behalf, so that we might become the righteousness of God in Him. (2 Cor 5:17—21)

I REMEMBER THAT MOMENT on a sunny Sunday afternoon in September 1972. It happened at a former resort a little south of Omena, Michigan on the Leelanau Peninsula north of Traverse City. (The last time I made my "pilgrimage" there, it had become an overgrown, unoccupied lot that had been for sale for several years.)

    That afternoon brought the culmination of the prayers of a school buddy, a "praying grandma," and a beautiful teenage girl who had been praying for her future husband, sight unseen, for the previous three years. That girl was Debbie Cousins, who would later become my wife of nearly forty-six years. (But she and I wouldn't meet for another year and a half, and that's another story.)

Lessons in Losing

That quiet Sunday afternoon I discovered for myself that God is real, and that He really does change lives. My life had for the previous few years been on a trajectory that was headed for a bad end. I wasn't in trouble with the law, but I was bitter and self-centered. I wanted to become a professional musician because it offered the kind of life that I thought I wanted—money, girls, dope, fame, seeing the world, and just lots of fun in general.

Ray, BC

Ray, AD

One of the things I love about the Lord is that He reaches out to us precisely at the place we are in life. He doesn't wait till we have reached a